There Will Be A Day

SONG BY JEREMY CAMP

ZONDERVAN®

ZONDERVAN

There Will Be A Day
Copyright © 2010 by Zondervan

Requests for information should be addressed to:

Zondervan, *Grand Rapids, Michigan 49530*

ISBN 978-0-310-51975-1

There Will Be A Day
Written by Jeremy Camp
Copyright © 2008 Stolen Pride Music (ASCAP) Thirsty Moon River Publ. Inc. (ASCAP) (adm. by EMI CMG Publishing) All rights reserved. Used by permission.

Cover design by Holli Leegwater | HL Design
Interior design by Holli Leegwater & Michelle Espinoza

Printed in China

09 10 11 12 13 14 15 • 20 19 18 17 16 15 14 13 12 11 10 9 8 7 6 5 4 3 2 1

There Will Be A Day

by Jeremy Camp

I try to hold on to this world with everything I have
But I feel the weight of what it brings, and the hurt that
     tries to grab
The many trials that seem to never end, His word declares
     this truth,
that we will enter in His rest with wonders anew

But I hold on to this hope and the promise that He brings
That there will be a place with no more suffering

There will be a day with no more tears, no more pain,
     and no more fears
There will be a day when the burdens of this place,
     will be no more, we'll see Jesus face to face
But until that day, we'll hold on to You always

I know the journey seems so long
You feel you're walking on your own
But there has never been a step
Where you've walked out all alone

Troubled soul don't lose your heart
'Cause joy and peace He brings
And the beauty that's in store
Outweighs the hurt of life's sting

I can't wait until that day when the very one I've lived for always
     will wipe away the sorrow that I've faced
To touch the scars that rescued me from a life of shame and
     misery, oh, this is why, this is why I sing …

There will be a day with no more tears, no more pain,
     and no more fears
There will be a day when the burdens of this place, will be no more,
     we'll see Jesus face to face

There will be a day
He will wipe away the tears
He will wipe away the tears
He will wipe away the tears
There will be a day

There Will Be A Day
—How the Song Came to Be

When Jeremy Camp talks about his faith there's genuine passion in his voice, and there's absolutely no question that he believes the lyrics to "There Will Be A Day" with all his heart. As with many praise songs, the catalyst was the writer's personal experience. Jeremy had lost his first wife to cancer eight years earlier, an event that tested his faith and resulted in a number of songs but "There Will Be A Day" sums it up the best. "It's a song of hope," he said. "It's saying, 'Don't lose heart; hold on.' We believers are going to heaven and we're going to see Jesus face to face."

Jeremy said the song came to him one night when he was driving home and listening to a radio broadcaster paying tribute to a certain individual. The broadcast made him think of the events that had shaped his own life and reminded him of Revelation 21:4—"God will wipe every tear from their eyes. There will be no more death or mourning or crying or pain, for the old order of things has passed away."

The lyrics just seemed to flow into his head as Jeremy drove. When he arrived home he got out his Bible to read Revelation 21:4 again. "Then I picked up my guitar and the song came out quickly," he said. "It was a God thing."

Jeremy emphasized over and over that a reward awaits in heaven, but his conversation with me was not one-sided. Jeremy takes a genuine interest in what others have to say. He's friendly and laughs easily and often. Most notably, though, he learned early in life that Christians can cope with anything because they always know "There Will Be A Day."

Steven Cole

I try to hold onto this world with everything I have
But I feel the weight of what it brings, and the hurt
that tries to grab

An anxious heart weighs a man down.

Proverbs 12:25

There is no man in the world without some trouble
or affliction, though he be a king or a pope.

Thomas A Kempis

Troubles are often the tools by which God fashions
us for better things.

Henry Ward Beecher

The many trials that seem to never end,
His word declares this truth,
that we will enter in His rest with wonders anew

Christ has turned all our sunsets into dawns.

St. Clement of Alexandria

My soul finds rest in God alone.

Psalm 62:1

Stop and consider God's wonders.

Job 37:14

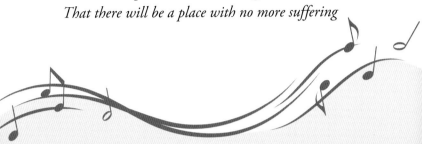

But I hold on to this hope and the
promise that He brings
That there will be a place with no more suffering

Jesus did not come to explain away suffering or remove it.
He came to fill it with his presence.

Paul Claudel

Jesus said, "The kingdom of heaven is near."

Matthew 4:17

Our citizenship is in heaven.

Philippians 3:20

There will be a day with no more tears,
no more pain, and no more fears
There will be a day when the burdens of this place
will be no more, we'll see Jesus face to face

Let us consider, beloved, how the Lord is continually
revealing to us the resurrection that is to be.
Of this he has constituted the Lord Jesus Christ the
first-fruits, by raising him from the dead.

Pope St. Clement II

Your face, LORD, I will seek.

Psalm 27:8

The glory of the LORD will be revealed,
and all mankind will see it.

Isaiah 40:5

But until that day we'll hold on to You always

Faith is nothing but a living, wide awake
consciousness of God within.

Mohandas K. Ghandhi

It is the Lord your God you must follow,
and him you must revere.
Keep his commands and obey him;
serve him and hold fast to him.

Deuteronomy 13:4

I hold fast to your statutes, O Lord.
Psalm 119:31

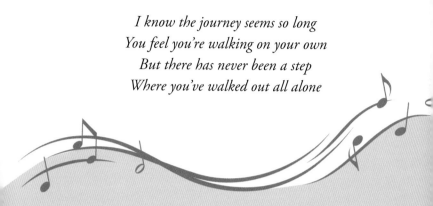

I know the journey seems so long
You feel you're walking on your own
But there has never been a step
Where you've walked out all alone

The eyes of the LORD are everywhere.

Proverbs 15:3

I will fear no evil for you are with me.

Psalm 23:4

Rejoice! … The Lord is near.

Philippians 4:4-5

Troubled soul, don't lose your heart
Cause joy and peace He brings

The Lord himself goes before you and
will be with you; he will never leave you nor forsake you.
Do not be afraid; do not be discouraged.

Deuteronomy 31:8

Joy is the most infallible sign of the presence of God.

Leon Bloy

We are all strings in the concert of his joy.

Jakob Boehme

And the beauty that's in store
Outweighs the hurt of life's sting

Jesus said, "Rejoice and be glad, because
great is your reward in heaven."

Matthew 5:12

One thing I ask of the LORD, this is what I seek:
that I may dwell inthe house of the LORD all the days of my
life, to gaze upon the beauty of the LORD.

Psalm 27:4

The only light upon the future is faith.

Theodor Hoecker

I can't wait until that day where the very one I've lived for
always will wipe away the sorrow that I've faced
To touch the scars that rescued me from a life of shame
and misery, this is why I sing …

The LORD is my light and my salvation.

Psalm 27:1

Surely God is my salvation.

Isaiah 12:2

My salvation will last forever.

Isaiah 51:6

There will be a day, he will wipe away the tears,
he will wipe away the tears, he will wipe away the tears
… there will be a day.

The day of the LORD is near.

Ezekiel 30:3

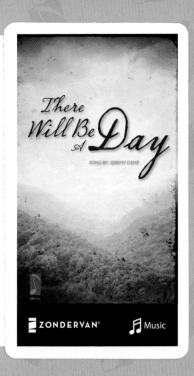

There
Will Be Day
A

SONG BY JEREMY CAMP

ZONDERVAN®   🎵 Music